SILENCE

A LOST TREASURE
in a
NOISY WORLD

"silent time"
Creative Quotations and Expressions
by
John H. Kappe

Houston, Texas

The "silent time" Creative Quotations and Expressions in this book are real if you believe them. Even if you don't believe them, they may, at least, stir a desire or two for silence in your life. Who knows, if you reflect on these "silent time" Creative Quotations and Expressions, they may even touch your heart and lift your spirit and who of us doesn't need that?

Silent Time: Creative Quotations and Expressions
Copyright © 2005 John H. Kappe
All rights reserved

Cover Design by Alpha Advertising
Interior Design by John H. Kappe
Typesetting by Pine Hill Graphics

Packaged by ACW Press
1200 HWY 231 South #273
Ozark, AL 36360
www.acwpress.com

The views expressed or implied in this work do not necessarily reflect those of ACW Press. Ultimate design, content, and editorial accuracy of this work is the responsibility of the author.

Library of Congress Cataloging-in-Publication Data
(Provided by Cassidy Cataloguing Services, Inc.)

Kappe, John H.
Silence : a lost treasure in a noisy world / by John H. Kappe. — 1st ed. — Ozark, AL : ACW Press, 2005.

"'Silent time' creative quotations and expressions."
ISBN: 1-932124-68-3   ISBN-13: 978-1-932124-68-2

1. Silence—Quotations, maxims, etc. 2. Silence—Meditations. 3. Quietude. 4. Solitude. 5. Peace of mind. 6. Quality of life. I. Title.

BJ1499.S5 K37 2005
306—dc22   0509

Printed in the United States of America.

Once upon a "silent time" in a noisy world I discovered that silence really is a treasure in my life. My hope is that, after reading this book, you too will discover what a treasure it is in your life.

Silence

Creative Quotations
and
Expressions
by
John H. Kappe

"silent time"

If you have a
moment,
be silent
and let the
"silent time"
fill your heart
and
lift your spirit.

Dedication

With love and fond memories, I dedicate this book to my loving parents, Henry and Melba Kappe. I also dedicate this book to my brothers and sisters, Betty, Barbara, Don, Linda and Mike, to my best friend, Daniel Guerra, Sr., to his parents, Oscar and Doris, and to all the people in my life who have spent "silent time" with me and taught me the value of sitting silently together, being together and loving together.

Most of the "silent time" Creative Quotations and Expressions in this book came to me in the silence. I must admit, however, that some of them were also born out of the noise and busyness of my life. So maybe silence and noise aren't such strange bedfellows after all.

"silent time"
Creative Quotations and Expressions

SILENCE

(ENOUGH SAID)

The illustration of the **Balloon**
is symbolic of
The Resurrection of Jesus.

The illustration of the **Lady Bug**
is symbolic of
*The Blessed Virgin Mary,
the Mother of Jesus.*

Contents

Introduction

To be able to be silent for a considerable period of time or, at least, to be able to steal away and capture even a few moments of silence in this day and age is an awesome accomplishment.

Choosing to be silent is an even greater accomplishment. All of us sometimes lose our drive for the silent side of ourselves, in lieu of getting caught up in a whirlwind of activity, trying to be all things to all people. Yet, while our quest for silence may seem an impossible task, we still make attempts at that awesome challenge. Sometimes we succeed at capturing a little silence in our lives here and there and sometimes we do not.

Silence, though it is often elusive, is nevertheless possible and it is always a gift. It is not a discipline and it is not a punishment. Least of all, silence is not an option for any of us who seek peace in a world filled with its share of stress and anxiety.

Silence is not easily experienced or achieved but it is always worth the effort. Any attempt at being silent has the potential to lead us to solitude and it is in the silence and solitude of our lives that we are most likely to encounter God and our true selves. Silence is one of those treasures that, in many of our lives, has yet to be fully discovered and appreciated. Unfortunately, many of us have suppressed the desire to be silent for so long that we find silence to be more a stranger than a friend. Consequently we are sometimes more awkward than comfortable in its presence. But once we begin to value that lost treasure called silence, we will appreciate it more and more for the balance it puts into our lives and for the peace it has to offer us.

There is no doubt that silence can be a two edged sword. It can be imposing and it can also be life giving.

If silence is a stranger to us, we will probably feel awkward and, perhaps, even uneasy in its presence. But the irony is that when we are successful at capturing significant "silent time" in our lives, even then, sometimes we don't know how to deal with it.

Consequently, silence sometimes makes us anxious but when we learn to be comfortable in its presence, it will also bring us peace and comfort.

Usually silence will not find us. We must be in pursuit of it.

At first, when we enter into the silence, it may seem deafening. Once we learn to sit with silence, and claim it as a welcomed friend, we will realize that it frees us to hear what the quiet has to offer us, and it will become a treasure that enriches us.

Once we become content in the silence, we will comfortably and willingly put aside, as secondary, all the other things in our lives that consume us and busy us.

We all have within us the opportunity and capacity to invite silence into our lives. Likewise, we have the power to suppress it. As long as we are content with the busyness in our lives, there will be no room for silence. But, once we choose to create a place for silence in our lives, we will discover that the busyness of life does little more than fill our time and distract us from pursuing the opportunity to live our lives on a deeper and more spiritual level.

Silence gives us freedom to see life anew and allows us the opportunity to re-prioritize the important areas of our lives that have become insignificant.

When we allow ourselves the freedom to become friends with silence, we will no doubt, be able to see life from an entirely new perspective. Perhaps then we will be able to introduce others to the silence within themselves.

The "silent time" Creative Quotations and Expressions in this book are partially the result of a silent day of prayer and reflection I made a few years ago at the Villa de Matel Convent in Houston, Texas. The following quotations and expressions – some fun, some serious, and some profound, may help you experience and appreciate silence in a whole new light. They may also help you to rediscover, once again, the value of silence in your life. For indeed, we cannot entertain silence unless we are willing to simply sit with it and be still. If we are willing to do that, we will come to a greater appreciation of silence and begin to experience a whole new quality of life.

To enter into the silence in a fast-paced society such as ours is no easy challenge. It is, however, a challenge that is life giving. So, I decided to speak up for silence in this book. I hope you enjoy these reflections on silence. My prayer is that they will take root in your life as they have in mine.

Father John H. Kappe

Acknowledgments

Four years ago I began the thought process for this book. Since that time I have written, compiled and edited the contents of these pages more times than I would like to admit. However, every word, every thought and every element of creativity has truly been a labor of love.

Though the thoughts, words, illustrations, quotations and expressions in this book are all my own, there are a number of people I would like to thank for their prayers, moral support and encouragement without which this book would never have been completed.

I am most grateful to my parents, Henry and Melba Kappe who have encouraged me for years to follow my dreams and to confidently use my gift of writing.

My gratitude also goes out to my friend, Daniel Guerra, Sr. for his gentle nudges that spurred me on to complete this work and for his confidence in me when, at times, I didn't feel like I could see the light at the end of the tunnel.

I also owe a debt of gratitude to Pat Morgan and Antoinette Winn who spent many, many hours typing and retyping the manuscript for this book and for sharing their creative genius on the computer.

I thank also all who believed in my ability to complete this work and encouraged me along the way.

I love you all.

In
the
secular world,
Silence
is often our
enemy.

In
the
spiritual world,
Silence
is   always
our
friend.

Silence
knows
no
words.
It is content
to let the
quiet
speak
for
itself.

Silence

is
to
our
spirit,
as
rain
is to the
earth.

Silence
is
born
of
peace, humility and acceptance.
The
Silent treatment
is
born
of
frustration,
fear
and
anger.

Silence
is
sacred,
even
when
the   truth
must
be
spoken.

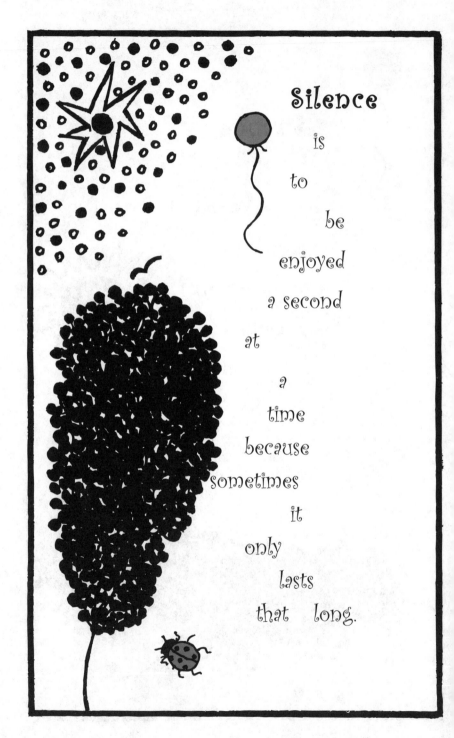

Silence
is
to
be
enjoyed
a second
at
a
time
because
sometimes
it
only
lasts
that   long.

Silence
can be
our
friend
or
our
enemy,
depending
on
how
we
embrace
it.

In
the
Silence,
we
can
hear
our
hearts
speak.

Sometimes those who are **Silent** say more than those who speak.

It is
so
self-righteous
of us to
think that we
have to say
something
about
everything.

Sometimes
it is
wiser
to
be
silent.

We
have
the
ability
to
break
anyone's
Silence.

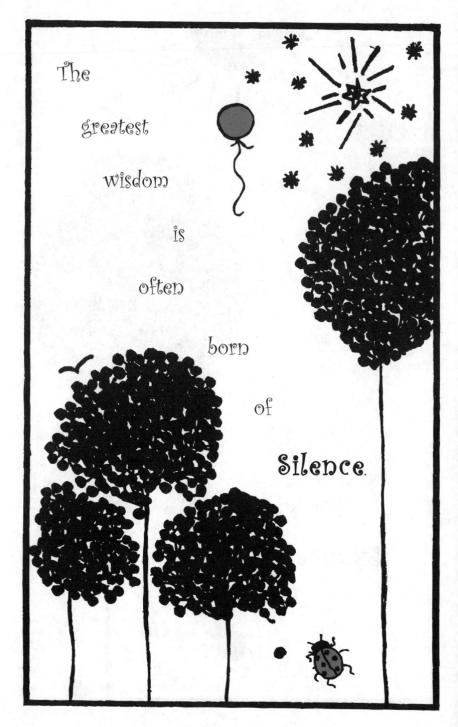

The
greatest
wisdom
is
often
born
of
Silence.

There

is

no

such

thing

as

a

Silent prayer.

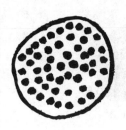

Silence
can
be
found
just about
anywhere –
in church,
in the park,
or in
our room.

But its real home is
in the recesses
of our hearts.

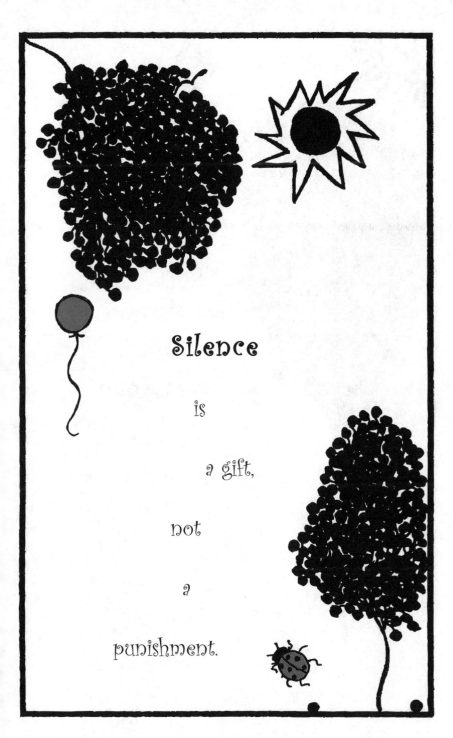

Silence

is

a gift,

not

a

punishment.

It is not
always
the noise
and chaos
from
outside of us
that invades
and interrupts
our **Silence**.

Sometimes
it is the noise
and chaos
within us that
is
the
culprit.

We often
forget
who we
really
are
until we
allow
ourselves
the freedom to
be
Silent.

41

Silence

is

the

language

of

the

heart.

Silence allows our minds the time they need to store wisdom.

Silence

is

not

difficult

unless

we think we

always have

something important

to

say.

When
we do
not
know what
to say
to someone,
perhaps
we should just
be **silent**
and let our
presence
speak for
itself.

Silence is not always
a discipline.
Sometimes it is
a gift
that no one
can give us
but ourselves.

So in this not so
Silent world, give
yourself the gift of
Silence,
and then you can tell
everyone
what a blessing
it really
is.

In the **Silence** of our lives, we need no words to speak to our hearts, to calm our spirits, to help us reflect on our lives, or to keep us in touch with who we are in life or in the face of death.

If we
are
uncomfortable
with
Silence,
perhaps
it is
because we
are
afraid to face
the
truth
about who
we
really are.

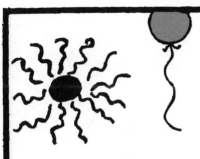

God is
Silent
when we speak
to Him in
prayer. Perhaps we
should
return the
courtesy and learn
to be
Silent
when God speaks
to us
in
prayer.

Expressing
our
prayers in
words
is
only
half of the
prayer experience.

Silence
is
the
other
half.

If
we
are
unable
to be **Silent**,
there is
no
doubt that
we
will also
be
unable
to
listen.

Once
we have
learned
to
cherish
and value
Silence,
we can
be certain
that
we have
made
peace
with
ourselves.

If, in our prayer,
we believe
that
God really
does come to us
in the
Silence, then
why do
we
spend so much
time
talking to God
and
telling Him
what
He already
knows?

53

Just
because
we are
Silent
does not
mean
that
we
have
nothing
to
say.

We

need to

put

more trust

in

the **Silence**

of our

thoughts than

in the

rambling of our

words.

For the
troubled
and the
broken hearted,
Silence
is
sometimes
a
burden
and
sometimes
a
blessing.

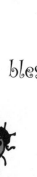

I once
thought
a
thousand
words
in the **Silence**
and
I am
proud
to say
that I never
spoke a one
of
them.

Verbal **Silence**

is

often

a

blessing

to

others.

Spiritual

Silence is

always

a blessing

to

ourselves.

A
Silent
reflection
is
never
a
wasted
moment.

If
we
can
remain **Silent**
when
we would
rather
speak,
we will
have
reached
a new
level of
maturity.

A
Silent
reflection
is
more
valuable
than
a
secret
thought.

The
greatest
thing
about
Silence is that
it is
a
gift that
we can
give
ourselves and
others.

Silence
has
the
power to
slap us into reality.

It also
has
the power to
allow
us
to
fantasize.

Sometimes
we
feel
alone
in the
Silence
and

sometimes
we
feel blessed
by
the
power
it
has to
enrich us.

Almost all things
    can be
appreciated
    in
    the
Silence,
        but
few things
        can
        be
        appreciated
        in
        the
        midst
        of
        noise.

We
need to
be
aware that
the lack of
Silence
in
our lives
is
sometimes
an intrusion
on the **Silence**
in
the lives of
others.

Silence

reflects
the
wisdom
and
peace
that
God
has
planted
in
our
hearts.

We
have
lost
something
of
great value
within ourselves
when
we
can no longer
sit
in
the **Silence**
and
be
content.

To be
Silent within
seems
an endless
battle,
but
if
we
can
win the battle,
we
will ultimately
find
peace.

No one

can

invade

and

respect

our

Silence

like

God.

To

sit

in

Silence

is

like

sitting

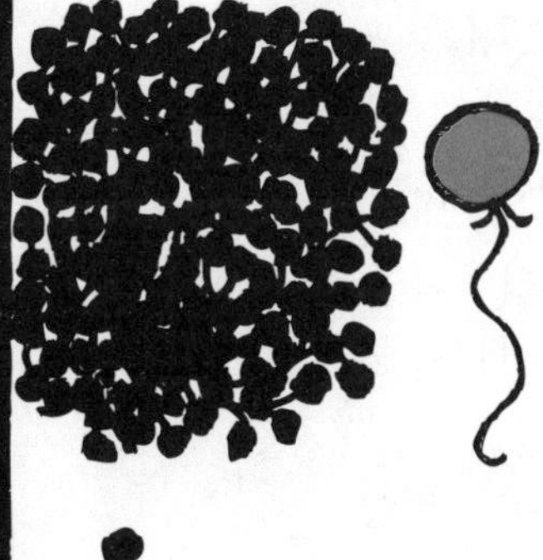

in   the

embrace

of

God.

Sometimes

our

Silence

is

a

greater

blessing to

others

than

to

ourselves.

Silence

is

often

abused

by

the

chatter of

unnecessary

words.

Silence

is

the

result

of

a

peaceful

spirit.

We

don't

have

to

go

anywhere in

particular

to find

Silence.

It

comes

from

within.

Sh – h – h -h!

Enjoy

the

Silence in

your

life and let

it

speak

to

you.

Sometimes

it

is

refreshing

to just

let

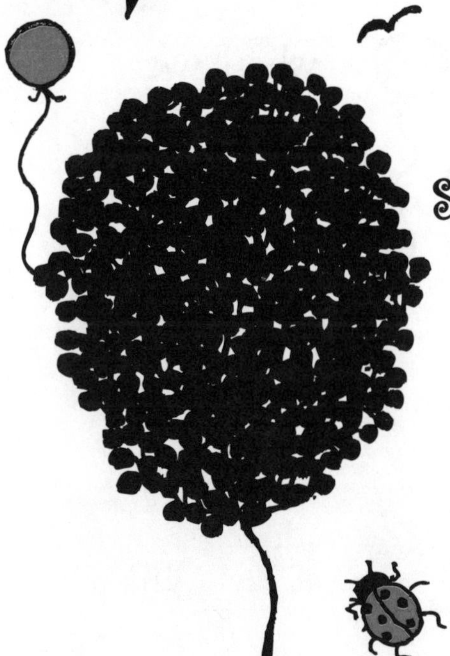

the

Silence in

our

lives

scream

at us.

We

can

only

appreciate the

value

of

Silence

when we

give

ourselves

permission to

claim

it as a

gift.

Creativity

    is

      more

        apt

      to

     be

born of **Silence**

    than

    of

brainstorming.

The

busy

me

is usually

what

I do,

but

the **Silent**

me

is who I

really

am.

I don't

care how

Webster

defines **Silence**.

It is

not

merely

the

absence

of

noise.

We

often

jabber

the

Silence

right out of

our

lives.

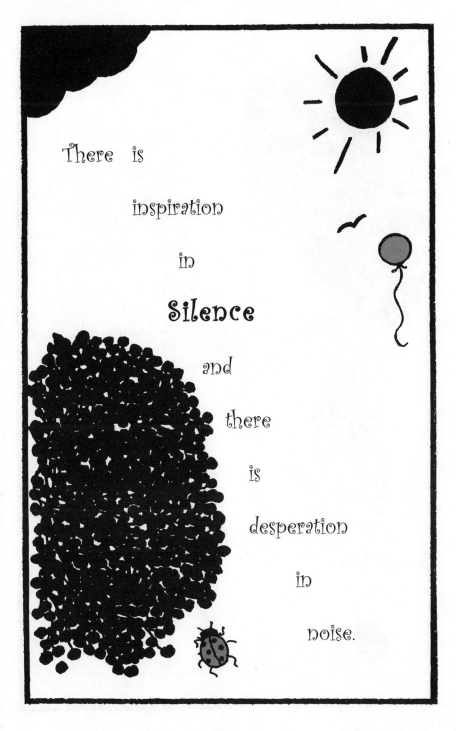

There is

inspiration

in

Silence

and

there

is

desperation

in

noise.

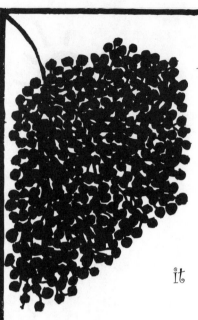

When

we

experience

Silence as a

discipline,

it is difficult.

When

we

experience

Silence

as

a

gift,

it is easy.

Our
Silence
is
often
broken
by others
and
other's **Silence**
is often
broken by
us.

When we are
speaking,
we can only
express one thought
at a
time.
When we are
Silent,
we can
entertain a
thousand
thoughts all at
once.

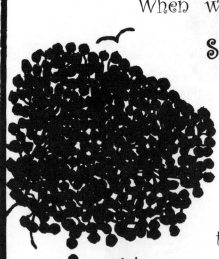

When we

allow

ourselves the

freedom

to be **Silent**,

everything

in our lives

looks different

and

feels

different.

When we
have
mastered
Silence
in our lives,
we will have
opened ourselves
to
learn things we
never knew
before.

It

is

wiser

to

be

Silent before

we speak,

than to

speak

foolishly

and

create

a

Silence.

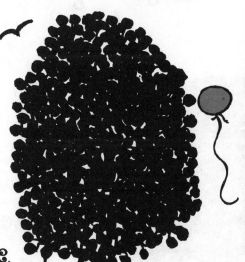

89

Some
people talk
all
day
and say   nothing
and
some people are
Silent all day
and speak
volumes.

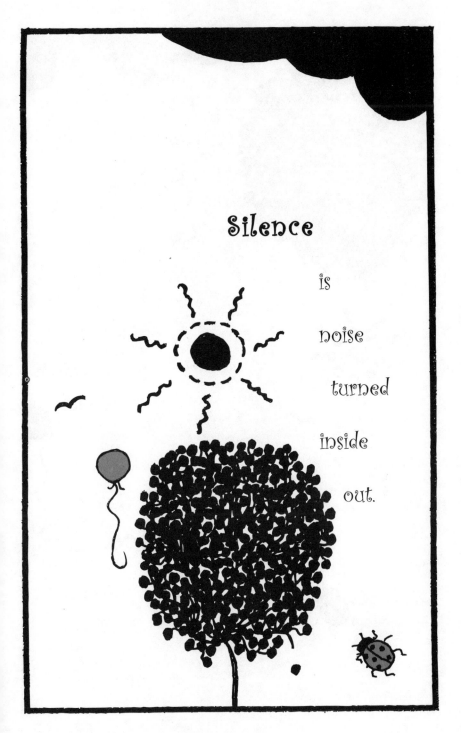

Silence

is

noise

turned

inside

out.

Someone

has

to

speak

up

for

Silence.

Silence

is

the

armor

of

prayer.

Silence
and
solitude
go
hand
in
hand.

When

we

come to

the quiet in

prayer,

we will never

find a

Silent God.

Silence

ignites

the

unspoken

prayer

within

our

hearts.

Silence

is

the

precursor

of

prayer.

God
often
calls
us in
the night because
that is when
we are most
Silent.

Don't
ever
be
Silent
in prayer
unless
you
really want to
meet
God
there.

Beware

of

Silence.

It is there

that

you will discover

who you

really

are.

Even

our

Silent

prayers

are

heard and

answered

by

God.

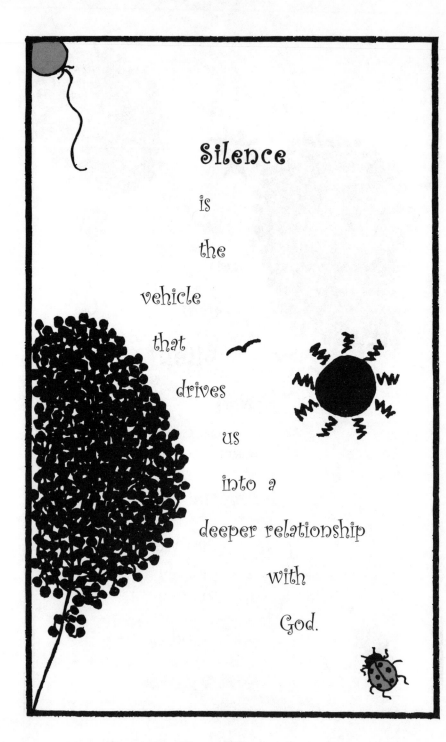

Silence

is

the

vehicle

that

drives

us

into a

deeper relationship

with

God.

Silence

is

critical

to

knowing

God

and

to

knowing

ourselves.

Even

when

God

is

silent,

He

speaks.

To be able

to be

Silent

in this day and age

is an awesome

accomplishment.

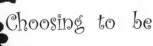

Choosing to be

Silent is

an

even

greater

accomplishment.

Sometimes we succeed

at capturing

a little

Silence in our

lives

and

sometimes

we

do

not.

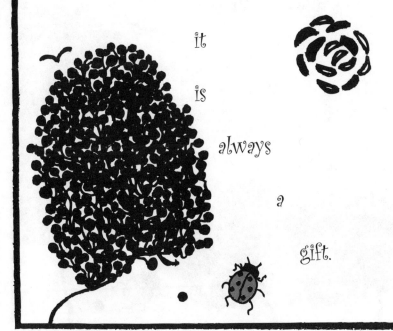

Silence,

though it is often elusive,

is

nevertheless possible

and

it

is

always

a

gift.

Silence
            is not an
                option
            for any of us
    who seek peace
    in a world
            filled with
    its share of
                stress
                and
    anxiety.

Silence

is

never

easily

experienced,

but

it

is

always

worth

the

effort.

Any attempt at being **Silent**

has the potential

to lead us to

solitude,

and it is in the

Silence and

solitude

of our lives that

we are most

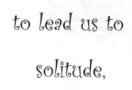

likely

to

encounter

God and

our true selves.

Silence

is one of those

treasures

in our lives

that has yet to be

fully

discovered

and

appreciated.

Many of us have suppressed the desire to be **Silent** for so long that we find **Silence** to be more a stranger than a friend.

When we

learn to

respect

Silence,

it will

put balance

in our

lives.

Silence can be a

two edged sword.

It

can be

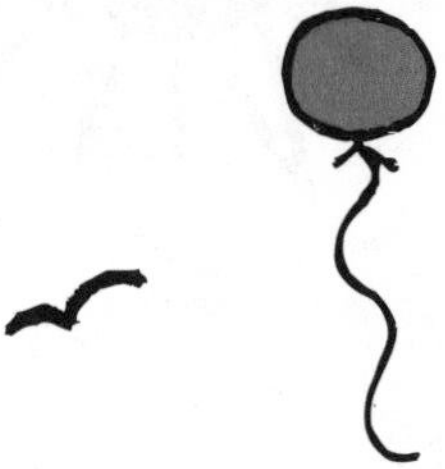

imposing

and

it

can

also be

life

giving.

If
Silence
is a
stranger to us,
we will
probably
feel
awkward,
and perhaps
even uneasy
in its
presence.

Usually

Silence

will not

find

us.

We

must be

in

pursuit

of it.

When

we

first

enter into

the

Silence,

it

may seem

deafening

to

us.

Once
we
become
content
in
the **Silence**,
we will
gladly
put aside
all else that
consumes us
and busies
us.

As

long

as

we are

content with

the busyness in our

lives,

there will be

no

room

for

Silence.

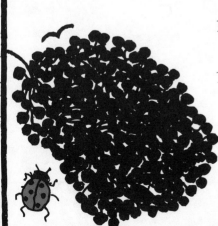

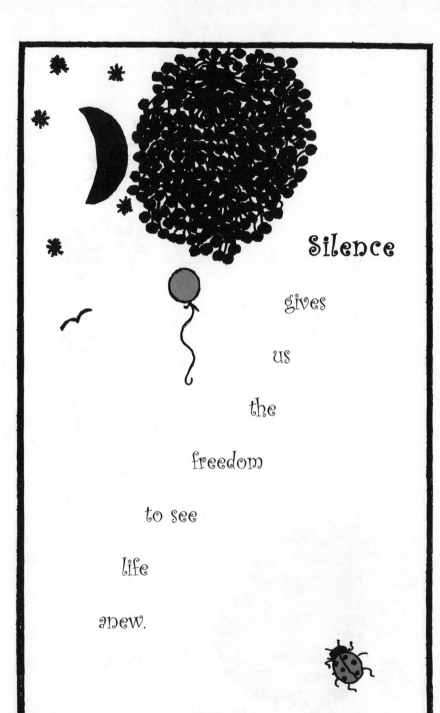

Silence

gives

us

the

freedom

to see

life

anew.

Silence is often

a curse to the

troubled and brokenhearted

and

a

blessing

to

the

peaceful.

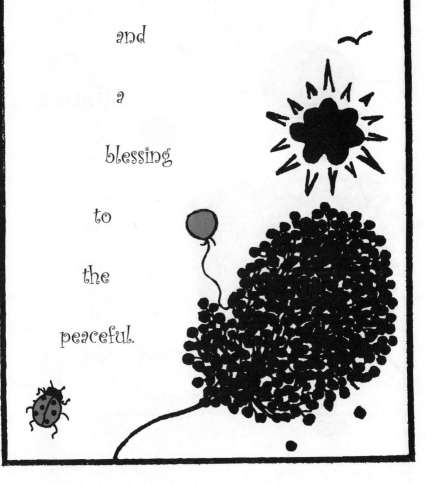

When we allow

ourselves

the freedom

to become

friends

with

Silence,

we will

no

doubt,

be able to see

life from an

entirely new

perspective.

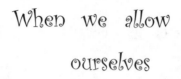

We

cannot

entertain

Silence

unless

we are willing

to

simply

sit with it

and

be

still.

To

enter

into

the

Silence

in a

fast paced

society such as ours,

is

no

easy

challenge.

More

people

ought

to be

willing

to

speak

up

for

Silence.

Silence

is

not

something

that

should

be

observed

only

in the

library.

A

Silent nod

can

mean as much

as

a

noisy

greeting.

Silence

can

even

fall

on

deaf

ears.

A

Silent

embrace

has

given

birth

to many

a

 relationship.

And

God

said,

"I will

come to

you

in the

Silence."

In the **Silence** of death, we are often taught the real meaning of life.

In the **Silence** of death

we are often most

aware

that life is a perishable

gift

that

is never

to

be

taken

for

granted.

In the **Silence**

of the death

of a loved one,

we are

compelled

to

collect

all of

the memories

of their

life.

Those who

really

love us

will sit

Silently

with us

in

our

moments

of

despair

and

confusion.

If we will

give

Silence

a chance,

it can

take

us on a

journey

to the

depth

of our

hearts.

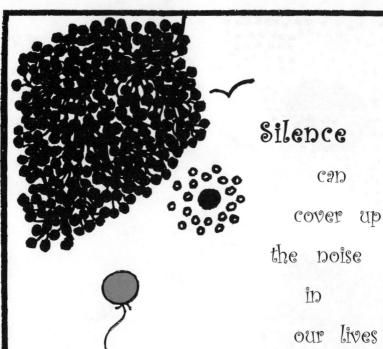

Silence
can
cover up
the noise
in
our lives
in the
same way
that noise can
cover up
the **Silence**
in
our lives.

Silence

is what

happens

when we discover

that having

the last word

is

not

the

most important

thing

in

life.

There
are
people who
feel a need
to speak up
and be heard,
and there
are
people who
are heard
simply by
their
Silence.

Even

the

slightest

whisper

can

break

the

Silence.

Sometimes

we

benefit

from our

Silence

and

sometimes

others

benefit

from

it.

Is

there

really such a

thing

as

a

Silent

majority?

In
the
Silence,
our
lips
can
rest
and
our hearts
can
speak.

A

Silent

memory

is sometimes

more

valuable

than

a

noisy

celebration.

Sleep
provides
us
with
the
Silent
time
we need
to
dream.

When
we break
the
Silence
of
the
morning,
we invite
a
new day
of noise
to
begin.

There

is

perhaps

nothing

more beautiful

than

the sound

of

Silence.

Some

    people

       know

         how to

be quiet.

Other people

   know

   how

   to

    be

      Silent.

Words

are

often

cheap.

Silence

is

more

often

valuable.

There

is

a

time

to speak

and

a time to be

Silent.

A
kind,
Silent gesture
can
heal
a
troubled
heart.

There

is

great

value

in **silence**,

especially

in

the

face

of

death.

Sometimes

even

the

deaf

do

not

know

Silence.

Many

creative

things

are

born

of

Silence.

Silence

can

be

deafening.

In
the
Silence,
anything
can
happen,
but
in
the noise
of life
we are
always
limited.

I
have
heard
some
amazing
things
in
the
Silence.

Part of me

has

learned

to be quiet.

All

of

me

must

learn

to be

Silent.

Quiet
and
Silence
are not
necessarily
s
y
n
o
n
y
m
o
u
s.

I used to think

when

people

were **Silent**

they

had nothing

to

say,

until I

realized

they were

probably just

listening

to their

hearts.

Sometimes

our

Silence

means

more to others

than

our

words.

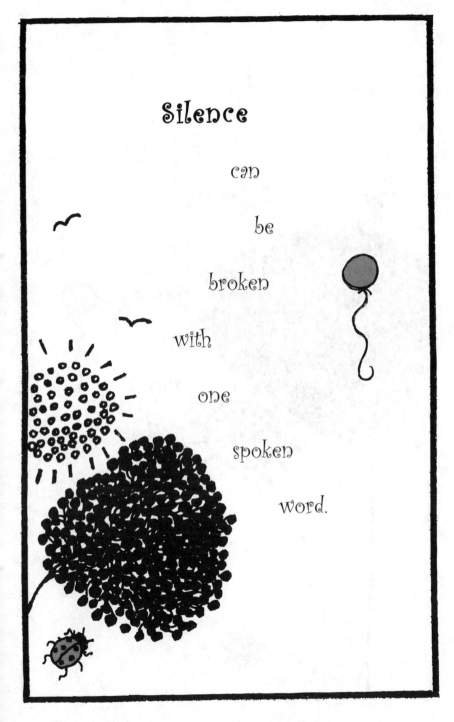

Silence

can

be

broken

with

one

spoken

word.

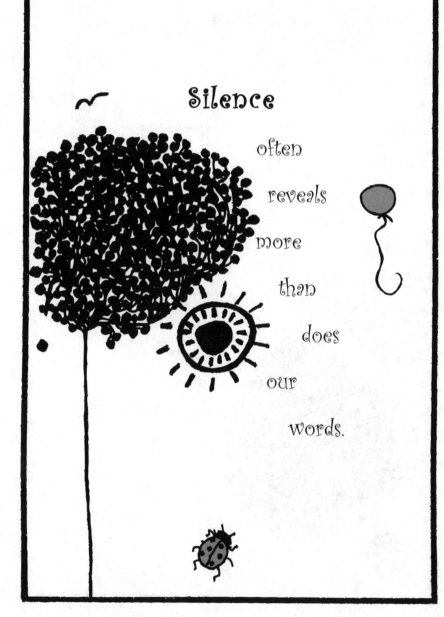

Silence

often

reveals

more

than

does

our

words.

I

used

to

think that

Silence was

merely the absence

of words.

Now I know that **Silence** is

the place where

God speaks

most loudly.

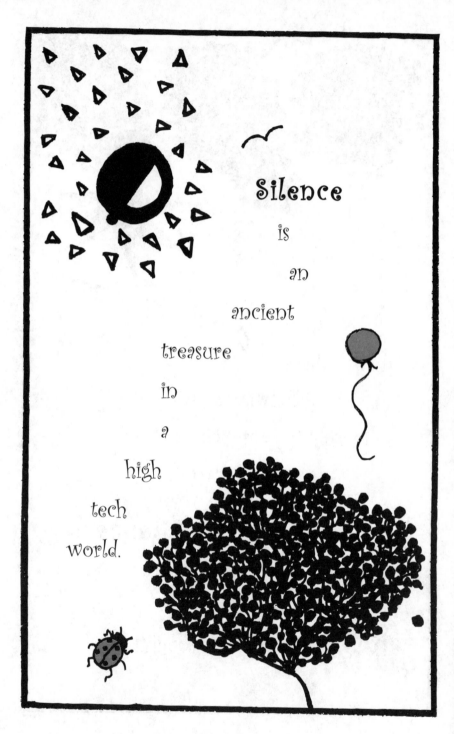

Silence
is
an
ancient
treasure
in
a
high
tech
world.

Silence
is
fragile
and
it is
easily
broken.

Silence –

everyone

needs

it

but

not

everyone

knows

they

need

it.

There
is
no
such
thing
as
a
Silent
God.

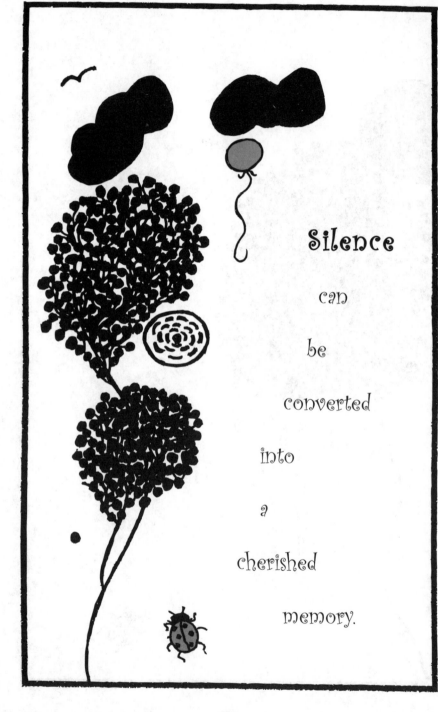

Silence

can

be

converted

into

a

cherished

memory.

Silence

is

a

friend

that many of us

have not

yet

learned

to

cherish

and

appreciate.

Silence
is
a
luxury
that
costs
nothing.

If it
is
true
that
Silent
waters
run deep,
I wonder
if it may
also
be true
that
noisy waters
run
shallow.

We
are
most present
to God
when we are **Silent**
and we
know that
it is in the **Silence**
that God
is
most present
to
us.

When we look
into a mirror,
we will see a reflection
of ourselves.
When we
are **Silent**
before God,
we
will discover
our true
selves.

Silence

is

a

nuisance,

and it is difficult

to attain

for those who

have an

opinion

on just

about

everything.

Silence
diffuses
the
noise
in
our
lives.

Solitude

is

where

Silence

and holiness

meet.

I'm

not

sure

that

Silence

can

be

described

with

words.

Words

are

wasted

on

those

who

love

Silence.

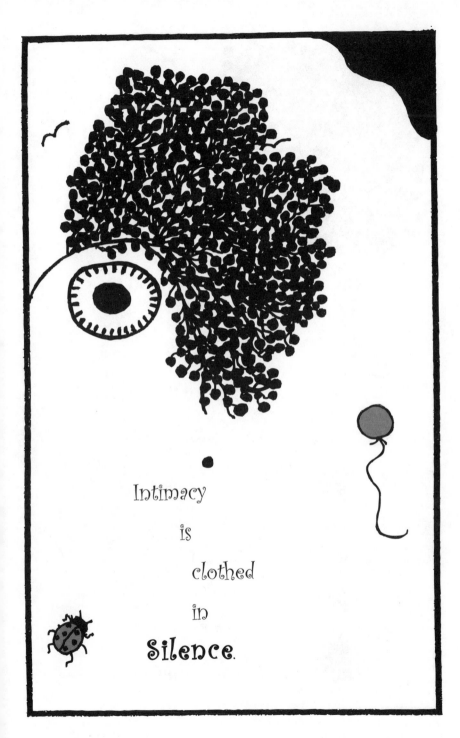

Intimacy

is

clothed

in

Silence.

In the

Silence,

we will discover

not only what

God sees in us,

we will also

discover

our own

self worth.

Silence

is

something

we

have to want

before

we can

possess it.

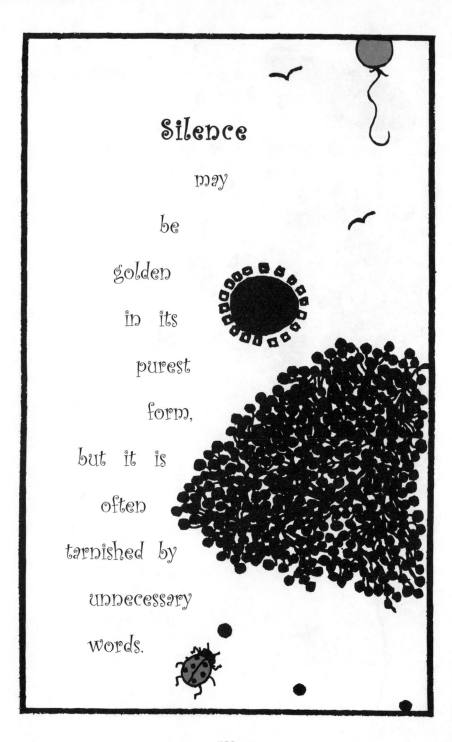

Silence
may
be
golden
in its
purest
form,
but it is
often
tarnished by
unnecessary
words.

Silence
is
a
lost
treasure
in
a
noisy
world.

If
we are
wise enough to
remain
Silent in the
presence of others,
they may
invite us
to speak,
and then
they will
listen to us.

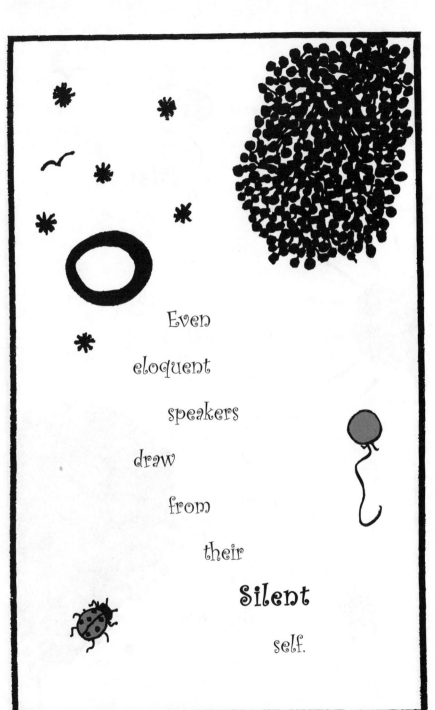

Even

eloquent

speakers

draw

from

their

Silent

self.

Silence
is
not
costly,
and yet
many
of us are
still
unwilling
to
pay
the price.

Silence

lies

deep

beneath

the

expression

of

our

words.

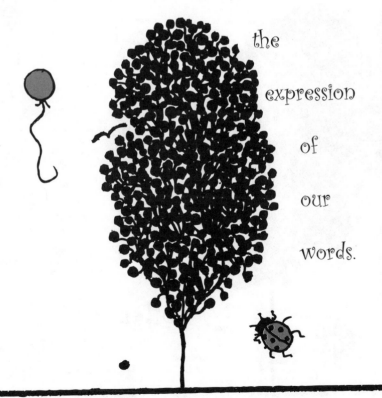

Churches
are
places
for us to go
so that
God
can
speak
to
us
in the
Silence.

Churches

are

often

Silent

so that

we can have

a quiet

place to

encounter

God.

Some people

force

Silence upon

us

by

not listening

to

what

we

have

to

say.

About the Author

Father John H. Kappe, a Roman Catholic Priest, was ordained May 22, 1971, and serves the Church in the Archdiocese of Galveston-Houston. He has always loved the creative side of his life and priestly ministry. Father John writes and appreciates art in all its forms.

Born in 1944 in Houston, Texas, Father John holds a Bachelor of Arts Degree and a Master of Divinity Degree from Immaculate Conception Seminary in Conception, Missouri.

After thirty-four years in the active ministry in the Roman Catholic Church, he continues to live in the Houston area and serves the Church as a parish priest, where he writes and creates "silent time" Creative Quotations and Expressions and fashions them into art.

About
"silent time"
Creative Quotations and Expressions

"silent time" Creative Quotations and Expressions are words turned into art. Each quotation and expression and each piece of art has a personality of its own.

The creative quotations, expressions and illustrations in this book are as simple as the silence from which they emerged. Yet they speak to our hearts and help us to value the new ideas that spring forth from them.

The "silent time" Creative Quotations and Expressions, all of the illustrations, and all of the artwork that accompanies this book, are the work of Father John H. Kappe. The book and the signed artwork are available to the public.

"silent time"
Creative Quotations and Expressions

Silence

A Lost Treasure in a Noisy World

is
printed
on

50-lb. high bulk, acid-free Vellum paper

Silence
Order Form

Postal orders: Rev. John Kappe
Our Lady of Lourdes Church
10114 Highway 6
Hitchcock, TX 77563

Telephone orders: 409-925-3579
713-829-3045

E-mail orders: <u>awinn@ololchurch.org</u>

FAX orders: 409-925-5094

Please send Silence to:

Name: _____

Address: _____

City: _____ State: _____

Zip: _____ Telephone: (_____) _____

Book Price: $18.50 + $1.50 tax

Shipping: $3.00 for the first book and $1.00 for each additional book to cover
shipping and handling within US, Canada, and Mexico.
International orders add $6.00 for the first book and $2.00 for each
additional book.